AF270592

NFL TEAMS

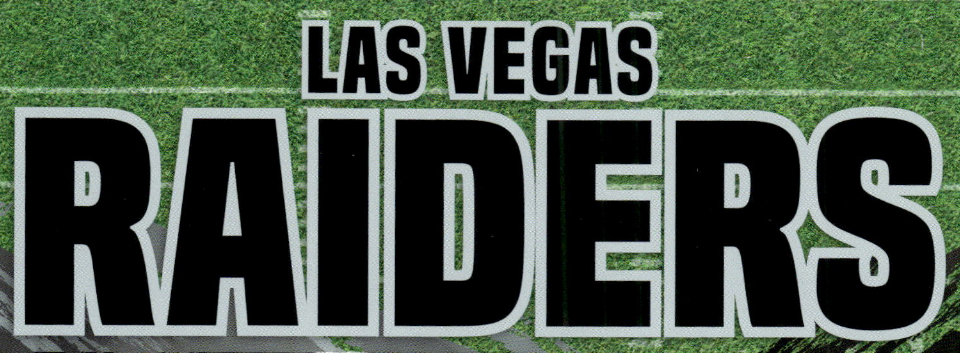

LAS VEGAS RAIDERS

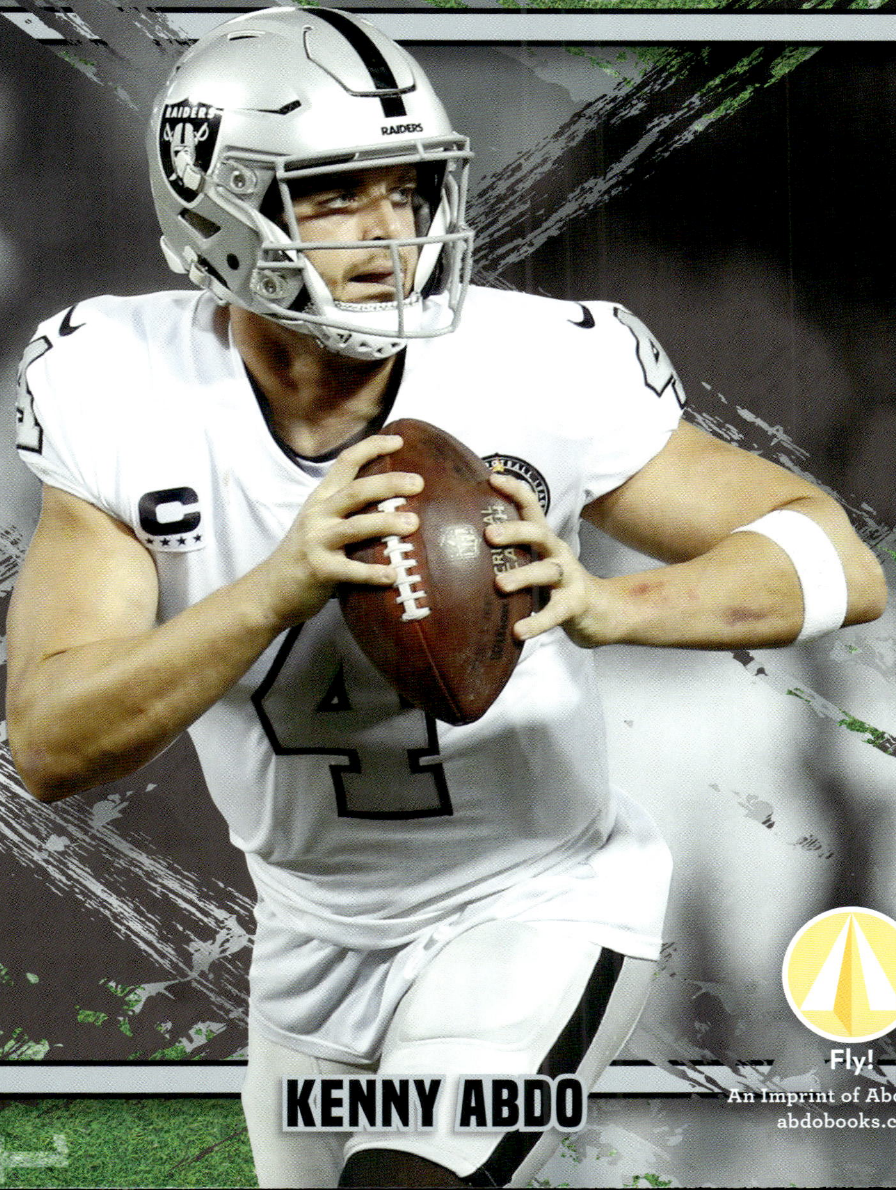

KENNY ABDO

Fly!
An Imprint of Abdo Zoom
abdobooks.com

abdobooks.com

Published by Abdo Zoom, a division of ABDO, P.O. Box 398166, Minneapolis, Minnesota 55439. Copyright © 2022 by Abdo Consulting Group, Inc. International copyrights reserved in all countries. No part of this book may be reproduced in any form without written permission from the publisher. Fly!™ is a trademark and logo of Abdo Zoom.

Printed in the United States of America, North Mankato, Minnesota.
052021
092021

Photo Credits: Getty Images, Icon Sportswire, iStock, Shutterstock PREMIER
Production Contributors: Kenny Abdo, Jennie Forsberg, Grace Hansen
Design Contributors: Candice Keimig, Neil Klinepier

Library of Congress Control Number: 2020919728

Publisher's Cataloging-in-Publication Data

Names: Abdo, Kenny, author.
Title: Las Vegas Raiders / by Kenny Abdo
Description: Minneapolis, Minnesota : Abdo Zoom, 2022 | Series: NFL teams | Includes online resources and index.
Identifiers: ISBN 9781098224677 (lib. bdg.) | ISBN 9781098225612 (ebook) | ISBN 9781098226084 (Read-to-Me ebook)
Subjects: LCSH: Las Vegas Raiders (Football team)--Juvenile literature. | National Football League—Juvenile literature. | Football teams--Juvenile literature. | American football--Juvenile literature. | Professional sports--Juvenile literature.
Classification: DDC 796.33264--dc23

TABLE OF CONTENTS

LAS VEGAS RAIDERS

With a long and exciting **franchise** history, the Raiders have proven to be a football team fans can admire.

As one of the original eight teams in the American Football League (AFL), the Raiders have conquered the homefield from Oakland to Los Angeles and finally Las Vegas.

KICK OFF

Oakland, California, was awarded a football **franchise** in 1960. The new team's first game was that same year. The Raiders finished their first season 6-8, but things would improve soon.

The Raiders had their first winning season in 1963 with Al Davis as head coach.

Four years later they played in **Super Bowl** II, but they lost to the Green Bay Packers 33–14.

The Raiders had advanced to within one game of the **Super Bowl** in six out of the next eight seasons. Following the 1976 season, the Raiders finally made it to another Super Bowl.

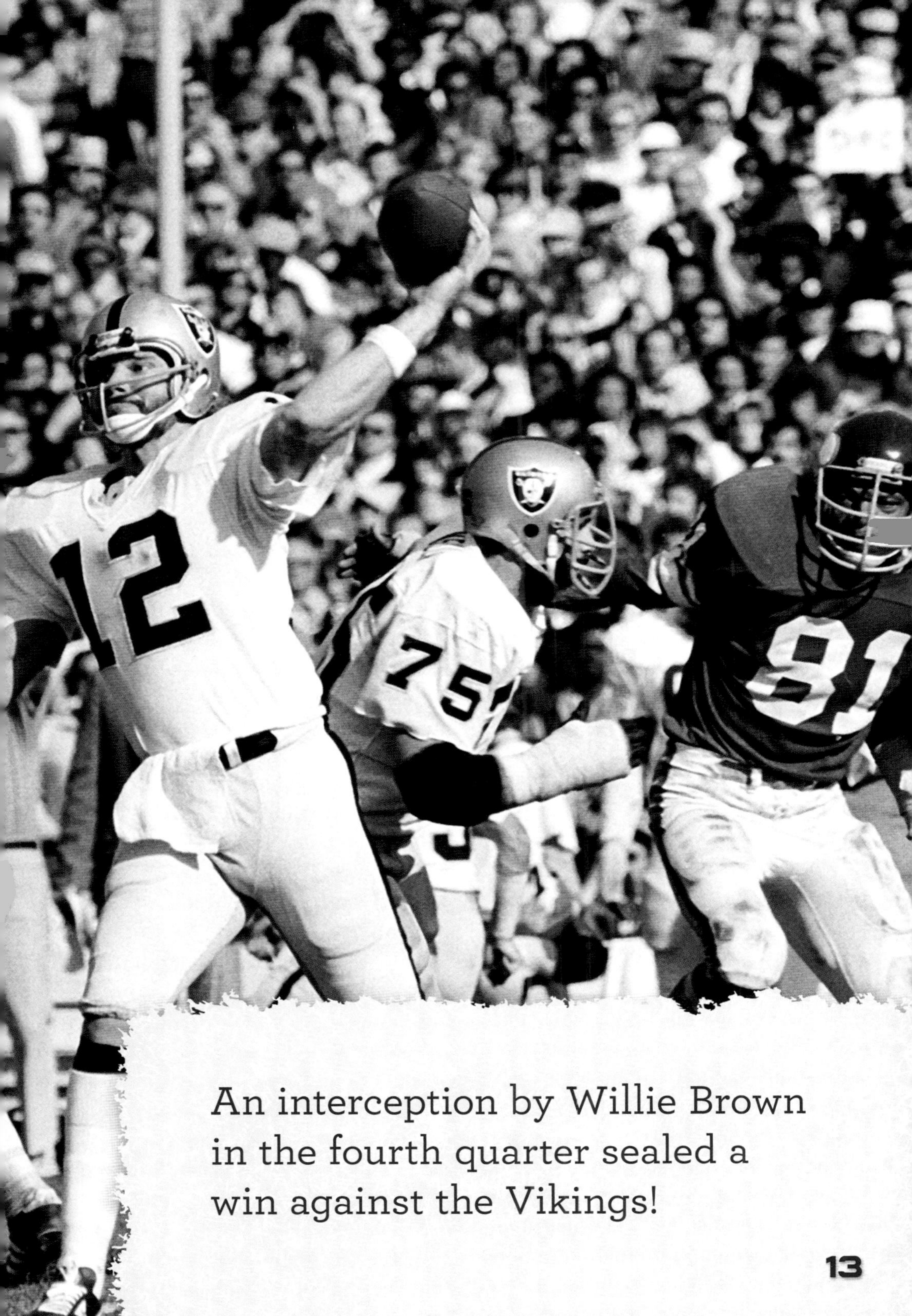

An interception by Willie Brown in the fourth quarter sealed a win against the Vikings!

TEAM RECAPS

The Raiders beat the Philadelphia Eagles at **Super Bowl** XV. **Quarterback** Jim Plunkett was named Super Bowl **MVP**! In 1982, the **franchise** made a big change. The Raiders moved from Oakland to Los Angeles.

The Raiders won **Super Bowl** XVIII against Washington 38–9. Running back Marcus Allen was named the game's **MVP**! Owner Mark Davis moved the Raiders back to Oakland in 1995 when he couldn't get a new stadium in LA.

The 2002 season led the Raiders to their next **Super Bowl** appearance. They lost to the Tampa Bay Buccaneers in a tough game 48-21.

The Raiders did not have much luck in the following years. They finished the 2018 season with a disappointing 4-12 record and the 2019 season with a 7-9 record.

Fabulo
LAS VEG
NEVADA
I LIVE IN NORTH DAKOTA
RAIDER
RAIDER NATION
RAIDERS

The Raiders moved to Las Vegas in 2020 after being in Oakland for over two decades. With a brand new stadium in lively Las Vegas, the team and its fans felt more good fortune was sure to come.

Wide Receiver Fred Biletnikoff helped the Raiders make it to **Super Bowl** II. He also helped win Super Bowl XI while being named **MVP**!

Biletnikoff had 589 receptions and 76 touchdowns with the Raiders. Biletnikoff was **inducted** into the Pro Football Hall of Fame in 1988.

Famed running back Marcus Allen helped the Raiders win **Super Bowl** XVIII and was named the game's **MVP**. During the 1985 season, Allen rushed for 1,759 yards and scored 11 touchdowns. He was named the NFL MVP that season! Allen was **inducted** into the Pro Football Hall of Fame in 2003.

FOOTBALL
ALL OF
CANTON
PRO FOOTBALL
HALL OF FAME
ENSHRINEE

Wide Receiver Tim Brown played for the Raiders for 16 seasons. Brown helped the team make it to **Super Bowl** XXXVII. During his career, Brown caught 1,094 receptions for 14,934 yards and 100 touchdowns. Brown was **inducted** into the Pro Football Hall of Fame in 2015.

GLOSSARY

franchise – a professional sports team.

induct – to admit someone as a member of an organization.

MVP – short for "most valuable player," an award given in sports to a player who has performed the best in a game or series.

quarterback (QB) – the player on the offensive team that directs teammates in their play.

Super Bowl – the NFL championship game, played once a year.

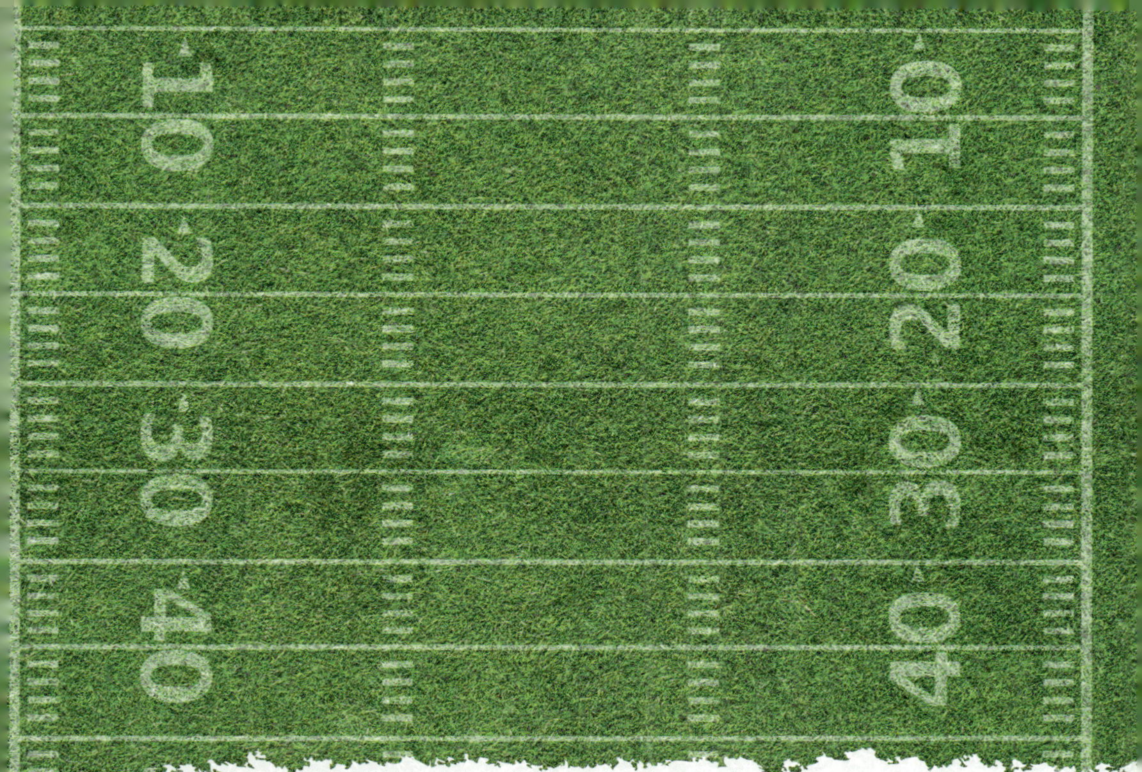

ONLINE RESOURCES

To learn more about the Las Vegas Raiders, please visit **abdobooklinks.com** or scan this QR code. These links are routinely monitored and updated to provide the most current information available.

INDEX